THE ME YOU DON'T SEE

Rochelle Melvin

THE ME YOU DON'T SEE

iUniverse books may be ordered through booksellers or by contacting:

iUniverse
1663 Liberty Drive
Bloomington, IN 47403
www.iuniverse.com
844-349-9409

ISBN: 978-1-6632-2560-3 (sc)
ISBN: 978-1-6632-2561-0 (e)

Library of Congress Control Number: 202191413420

Print information available on the last page.

iUniverse rev. date: 06/30/2021

Contents

Her She

It's a dark feeling that comes over me that I sometimes feel. It's angry and sad, and my joy has somehow lost its appeal.

Going around in a repetitious circle of clattering in my head are the many things I can't seem to forget.

Questioning always who I am and why I am here, feeling all this pain, the very loneliness I fear.

I fantasized we'd be together forever, you and I. I thought we would never part until the day I kissed this life goodbye.

Was any of it truth, or was it all merely lies, the if, the when, the sometimes
I love you? And why?

What was the point, and why were you ever there, only to leave me on the line, clothed in my seemingly permanent despair?

My heart hurts every day, and all the time I carry it like a part of myself, something I can't leave behind.

It pains me to swallow, even to breathe. Why oh why, my love, did you have to leave?

You left me yearning for your touch, the whisper of your smile. I say every day, darling, and all the while,

This is no good. This thing has to find an end. It's time for me to start over and begin again.

Pretty Girl

Pretty girl, you're not so pretty at all. Harsh and cold inside, you're as brittle as the fall.

Your mouth is alluring, beautiful, an invitation, a trap. Masked you are in a perfume as adhesive and sticky as sap.

Never caring whom you hurt or about the carnage you leave behind, you simply move on, leaving your widow's scorn with a death toll that goes on, etched in time,

A time that creeps with no measure, stealing lifeblood, leaving not a pleasure.

Sad faces, smileless hearts, and broken wings. Breathing no longer cherished, not by any living thing.

What was once a celebration now suffers in the darkness. Nary a glimmer of hope, just utter and terminal blindness!

Slave

I am in a web that I cannot seem to find my way out of. My arms and my legs are no good to me, helplessly dangling about.

I scream, but no one hears me. I speak, but my words only bounce back at me.

I have cried so long that my tears are no more. My back aches, and my throat is sore.

Every day I wonder what I have done wrong to be sitting here singing my sad, sad song.

No matter how hard I try, I can find no clear answer, just loathing, a gun, and remnants of that damned cancer.

I walk and I'm forever by myself, trying to escape a world of continuous self-doubt.

My cell is a prison of blood-soaked fleshy bars, a broken existence baying heavily at the stars.

For relief daily I do pray, for some semblance of my former self and its familiar way.

I question how so much grief can consume one being, filling me from head to toe with all I'm seeing.

It is a misery as known to me as the betrayal of a onetime friend and a visitor more deadly than all of sin.

Forever withered is that free and eloquent spirit of mine, now gone, leaving the tattered pieces of what once was behind.

Broken

I've been crippled for very long, but now that I can walk around, I find that the whole world, everywhere—every place—is shut down.

I'm trapped inside my house. They shout, "COVID! Don't go out!" when all I want to do is spread my wings and shout.

I want to dance, walk, and run crazily about—take as many steps as I choose with no doubts—

Only to wear my soles thin, my feet bare. O to know an amazing freedom and all that I dare.

Ominous, the Rewrite

Hate is a liar, a killer, and a thief;
The darkest of figures, the black seat;

Anguish, misery, and so much pain; deception, trial, and never a single gain;

Joylessness; a lacking on the inside; strife, destruction, and dear misplaced pride.

A rage fills their faces; their lips do not smile. Deep down inside lies the bitterness of a bellyful of guile.

Long-suffering, anger, heartlessness, and disillusion. War and death. Battles, they have no conclusion.

Hate is prejudice, bigotry at its worst, caring for none this murderous curse.

Hate is the creeper, quiet and cunning, its continuous motor steadily running.

A killer, a liar, and a thief, you see, ripping away at all the good inside of us.

The predator, a succubus, the false king, the hater, and the devourer of everything.

The monster in your nightmares, and two steps behind, a wicked maze of terror seeking always to find.

Reverse if Only

Girlfriend, I can't replace the poetry. You stole my years, my youth, and my happiness—God's truth.

The child I lost, the sadness and time endured, the friends and former relations procured.

The glimmer in my eyes cannot be restored. Either can the slimmer waist or my tight athletic vibe.

The tenderness in my heart can't be revised, and neither can the regret I feel that you were ever a part of my life.

Girlfriend, I gave you my key, gave you the marrow, the greatest slice of me.

Though you threw it all back in my face while you laughed, you're taking much more than half.

What a monster you are, and one you shall always be, cutting, cutting evermore at the core, the whole of me.

Your cruel words harshly dance about. Your giggle, your spite, speaks volumes; it does shout.

So cold you can be; you strike like a jolt. But it was too late—yes, too late—for me to bolt.

Locked in, shut down, and helpless for your kiss, I—only God knows—really didn't sign up for this.

Sin

We have read about you in the headlines, watched your bloody hand across our TV screens,

Visited what your merciless affliction hath unwound, your shattering of the brightest gleam.

The heavy nails of impatience rigid and cold, knowing no guilt, no consequence.

Your reign in the endless story, incomplete yet foretold, the documentary of all this foolishness its meaning.

Though carrying truths does burden our youth, upon their backs they bear their predecessors' weight,

Never sure of the many proven truths, their feet are entangled in the barbed wire of lies' gait.

As a lion with two heads this system devours, slowly then swiftly as moments pass,

Each one having fewer hours, ticking away, dumping its remains like trash.

No mercy spared, and the end is close at hand. No olive branch dared, but we must make a way to start again,

To heal what is broken and to make well, or else we're all doomed. I'm not joking—straight to hell.

Fantasy

The faint but brilliant laughter echoes throughout the land's chamber, its sounds saturating, bouncing off every wall.

Joy's replenishing essence and the tone it holds. No danger bursting through the seams. The sheer beauty of its call.

The sun is a candle bringing the brightness to the day with warming impressions. His hand meets our cry.

Upon every tolerating rooftop his beams play, presented as a perfect picture high in yonder skies.

The old oak, she smiles, bathing, nourishing every branch, every leaf grown. And the breeze, it comforts her as a babe in its mother's arms.

A paradise surrounding me, hidden yet known, all that is majestic and beautiful sparing no charm.

Shock and awe 'tis the music, the melody, playing. Bluebirds and cascading waterfalls plunge toward the rocks below.

In a dream I knew what the earth was saying, this bounty of vision capturing me, the sun's watchful eye a charm more precious than anyone can ever know.

The Creature Within

Surrendering to the madness, my body swims through waves of muck and mire. Burning my flesh to the bone, this blaze of crimson fire.

There is no retreating; the influence is too strong. It feels so right, but we know it's wrong.

As does a cancer, you're eating me alive. I cannot think or move. I dare not thrive.

In a circle continuously going round and round. In the air one minute, my teeth carving the ground in the next.

Distorted, my breaking appearance. I flee its ugliness, avoiding the mirror, frightened of what I might be.

Who am I, this creature I've become? There are horns protruding from my skull. See these razor-sharp and venomous thumbs?

A monster and a criminal at large. Please arrest me; I accept my charge.

It's Cancer

A red liquid flows through me, spilling across the pavements of my life. My skeleton flies above me like bees escaping their hive.

I fashion my skin from the inside out, exposing all my nerves very clearly and without doubt.

I am simply a body bending, as limp as a wind-up doll, one that has lost its luster, its mechanical know-how.

Desperate breaths ascend from its essence. A lively charge is required, a needed upload. Maybe even a handy screwdriver.

What is broken is hanging by a thread, a girl, a boy, who thinks he or she is better off dead.

There's no repairing what is shattered upon the floor—no fix-it shop or hardware store.

Simply pick up the pieces and dispose of them, please. Then lock all those windows and return the keys.

Rid the blood of this wretched deadly poison. You see the stranglehold it has on me, my undeniably owned self-pity.

To move past these oceans of illness in waves, to embrace the wellness the body so craves.

No Title

Like clockwork, the moments tick away the hours, giving rise to a new day as they pass.

But when the heart throbs and is painfully sullen, the hours turning into days become horribly daunting,

A constant reminder of the hurt suffered, the disappointment of lost love boldly uncovered.

Someone once said that pain heals with time, but I beg to differ.
The pain only seems to swell, more determined, in the channels of one's mind,

Growing more pronounced, this culmination of one's displeasure. And it marks a time that creeps, attaining not any lost treasure,

Just more hours to think and more days of sadness. But there is no turning back of time's clock,
No going back to what was once had.

Grave

Death, death, death. His raspy voice
Calls thee. Far off but ever so near, yes, he beckons me,

Inviting me to his definite permanent slumber, yeah, without a single
care for what death means, what it does encumber.

Death is the ending, the suspension of all that I have known, the years,
the tears, and my privilege ever grown.

Death's cold fingers lie against my unwilling shoulder blade, taunting
me with his games, those games well played.

I stand far from ready to engage with my breath's end. I'm not willing
to concede, to accept dust's brazen win.

No, I will not lie down and be a smorgasbord for the worms. I want to
live forever under no uncertain terms.

I am avoiding the silk-lined fabric of the pine box that eagerly awaits
my body—or the body of those young or old, those big or small, that
of just anybody.

The grave, the grave, the grave opening its ample mouth, enveloping
the uncountable number of bones rattling in this death house.

The grave gives passage to another place. It is the place where death
repeats the end of all days.

Innocence

The world is falling down around me, and war is as common as the cream in my tea, but still outside I hear children's laughter, infectious as only laughter can sometimes be.

They play happily with their toys without a care in the world, their joys involving the simplicity of being a young boy or girl

Shielded from the weighty sufferings around them that bind, their only concern being the bogeyman in the closet who in their dreams they never find.

Such freedom brings to mind those days of youth, swinging from the branches in the woods upon that black spruce.

O tender days of youth, what a gift you be. Again to see the world through the dear eyes of thee,

To appreciate the aroma of every summer's day while exhausting the waves of bliss, joyous celebration at play,

And to witness the innocent glimmer of wonder in the children's eyes, the warmth of liveliness, the exuberance of daily surprise.

Childhood's breath. Children should know no burden, but to the sweet song of angels should the children hearken.

Beautiful One

Through my window, I look across the alleyway. She's smiling, playing with her long hair that way. She's often styling.

I imagine the sweet, sweet scent of her cool breath. I marvel at the sleek curves of her youthful breast.

What a beauty. A perfect woman she shall forever remain. Her features' exquisiteness should be always the same.

Her laugh is like a lovely song well sung; her words, a sonnet, another brilliant poem.

And even in a field filled with weeds, her flowery presence will always proceed.

Making desolate and ugly places gleam with bright and glorious graces,

Her dear silhouette is something special to behold. It is a story, a conversation, in my memory again and again told.

She is my angel and all my beautiful dreams come true. She sends my mind soaring as high as a kite in flight.

Though I cannot reach her or touch her, I believe she feels me. She feels me imprinted on her heart as deeply as she feels her blood flowing in her veins.

Loving this beautiful creature is a wonderful thing. My love makes me free and gives my spirit amazing wings.

Beautiful, beautiful, beautiful one, you cannot know my pleasure. How does your mere image give this lonely soul a joy that I cannot measure?

No, not by its width or its length, or even its weight, but like infinity, it forever has no end or set date.

Darkness and an Abiding Ghost

The watchful eyes in the darkened eve stare. A dull and lonesome sense chatters.

The essence of the creeping night utters "Beware" as every heartbeat sounds *pitter-patter.*

I dare not be a victim; on this you can bet. Though I fear I'm the subject of a fright undenied.

Strange and eerie shadows about the venue, with pillow-like footsteps, glide,

Owning this darkness, presenting such a horrid adventure. But by day, above the basements rafters they hide.

Heartbeat

I can hear my heart beating. It skips a pace twice, informing me of all that is missing, all that is denied in my life.

Challenging is my every day. My thoughts go on. I wonder, *Must I suffer the dawn of a new day unborn?*

Thump goes my heart, assuring me that I'm alive, that my blood races through me, and that I must abide.

It tells me that I must take another step, breathe another breath, know love's impulsiveness and never forget.

It reminds me of one much greater than I who sits on a throne high in the bluest sky,

The conductor of every beat of my heart, the orchestra man of the symphony playing in my life's spark.

I'm compelled to listen to the tempo of this heart beating with lively gratitude every day until the day of its timely ceasing.

Aquatic Reflections

A reflection of starlight kisses a raging sea, and waves batter the awaiting shore. Day breaks as seagulls dine on urchin above the seafloor.

A single shell pierces my heel, the shell hidden slightly below the many beds of sand. I can feel the warmth of God's mighty breath and hear the ocean's power at his mighty command.

Angelic beings dwell here, majestic, and nary a one of them is the same. I sit here watching this watery paradise as I consider each resident by name.

The blue whale, the shark, the jellyfish, the starfish, and even the walrus all have a certain appeal. The arctic creatures include a famous mammal, the silky-skinned black seal.

They rule the massive oceans, or at least their girth so implies, with a wisdom that will outlive the ages. The story of these giants has been told, often while turning pages.

Monumental walls made of sand and stone glisten with stems of green algae. This aquatic plant speaks to me as far as mine eyes can see.

What a collage, a magnificent parade of multicolored brilliance.
My every viewpoint holds significance to my heart's
Contentment, so gloriously convinced.

Angry Love

Love isn't always all Cupid and heart-shaped arrows soaring about. No, sometimes it's madness, a storm, and raging steel raindrops that shout.

Not always dinner and soft candlelight, but more like a severed heart's frustrations with nothing going right.

Sometimes it seems that the harder you try, the worse it gets, bidding for another person's attentions, his or her love, while keeping your own self-respect.

You wonder all along, *Why didn't I go, get away?* Maybe because steadily something inside you is begging you to stay.

Not the rough fists that meet your flesh, or even how your partner's love and cruelty never meshed.

Not that many hours have you sat waiting for a call. Even so, many times you simply put up with it all.

Love isn't always all Cupid and heart-shaped arrows soaring about. Sometimes it's mailing back the keys and walking out;

Loving yourself when no one else can, or so you think; picking yourself up; and becoming your own best friend.

Secrets

Sensing a stirring when I hear your voice, I cannot sleep when you're not here.

I'm in love with you, and I have no choice: to be away from you is something I cannot bear.

You have corrupted me and my whole presence, spoiling me for the rest.

I want to make love. Though you are hesitant, your feelings I need not guess.

You call me a child every time I pout. I look to you with an eager questioning.

It's time for me to find out all that I seek. The not knowing is punishing.

I must have you, your attention, and your every thought, you being the catalyst to my madness and every lesson taught.

Fake

Always claiming to be a person you are not. Hiding for so long the real you, who you are is something you have forgot.

You were never satisfied with who God made you to be, wearing that fake self so well. You're a chameleon, true blue.

You believe that people like you more when you pretend, but why do you believe these poseurs are your friends?

They don't see you, only your mask. The face you wear is as fragile as glass.

Hey, phony, you're not real like wax. You are brittle, so easily broken, and those people are not your ride-or-die; you're just their token.

They're only there for the perpetrator you are, the person you pretend to be. When was the last time you questioned "Who truly gives a damn about me?"

You're a liar living your life on borrowed time, but there'll come a day when your true identity arrives,

Relieving you of that person untrue there standing before your eyes, and opening up the world of "Wow, it's really you."

No more burden, no mask, no pretending. There's a fresh new start, a new life beginning.

Silence of the Casket

This quiet is very loud, speaking in deafening whispers. Its words are bold, cold, and solemn yet clever.

Mostly dismissing all that is fear, they brandish a solitary wit like a badge, one not so dear.

I am calculating my displeasure as it steadily mounts, yet I sense a pitiful gain at my despair; ears that do not hear do not count.

Loneliness loosens its jaws to eat, chewing on the bones, savoring my meat.

I long for the quality of noise now so far out of reach. A costly lesson does this damned solitude teach.

Alive

I now have hope for a brighter day,
Faith in a better way,
My joy fueling my stay.
No more wallowing in Satan's decay.
Reveling in God's Word, his say,
Like a small child, my spirit is at play
Doing the Lord's work and how I may.
My heart is now at peace when I lie down at the end of the day.
Every morning I pick up my Bible without delay, and throughout my days I'm content; I'm gay.

As He walked

As he walked, he saw a plane soaring past overhead. He wondered what its destination was and what would happen if it were to fall from the sky like lead.

He watched the many people as they went to and fro in their respective workplaces, seeing the tired smirks on their faces.

Their combined thoughts could fill a sea, and their patience filters were dangerously overwhelmed.

As he walked, he met a guy who introduced himself as a manly Terrence sort. He was nice, though almost bursting with neighborly advice.

Still as the first man walked, he listened to the cracking melody, the sounds of the brown leaves beneath the hard rubber tip of his cane, the sound delightful because his legs had now conquered the once forbidden task of the simple moving of his body's train.

But mostly as he walked, he enjoyed the solitude and meditated on what would be his next rhyme.

As he walked, there was no diminishing, no bad consequence, just great moments spent alone at his own joyous expense.

A Place

Look at those clouds of white in that sky, which goes on, it seems, into a forever that is very vast.

The trees are a rich brown with leaves very green; the darling scent sings with effervescence.

And a fellow sits in his wheelchair staring upward, taking in all the splendor, while a hound takes a whiz, and a squirrel, with a smile, in the trash plunders.

Many nostrils inhale the dear fragrance of the fresh mornings, the break of day. Eyes admire the surface of the creek and its almost musical swaying.

A bow-legged pigeon finds his mate as this Sunday morning slows down as if it has no time, no particular date.

Prayers bounce off every crevice of my street. Folks are all dressed up in their best. My, they look so neat

Marching practically in uniform as they enter our church, anxious to find the Word inside them, which is what they are all searching for.

Despair

Despair fills all the spaces in one's mind, the joy shredded like so many strangling vines.

It's the death of everything, the birds, the flowers, the creatures of the sea.

The end of days follow human beings ever closely, but still they do not see.

Seeping in is the taste of blood formed daily in the mouth. Tired, weary-eyed, people lie, hardly able to be roused,

Afraid that in their slumber, destiny will call in its debt. Therefore the game of life has lost its bet.

Teetering on the sharpened edge of a bladed sword, they are nearing absolute annihilation and its daunting reward.

No one wants to truly know their fate, the predetermined place where they will come to rest, knowing that they haven't met the requirements of the place that is best.

An empty desolate house is what I call their inability to feel. It is a house where love is vanquished, further sealing the enemy's deal.

They find pleasure in what is not good, and their faces wear a scowl that says, *Please remove this if you would.*

Lift me from these chains of indifference, and save me from the arresting stronghold of silenced footsteps.

Give me the words. Let them form on my lips that I might verse the proper and righteous wit.

Sing the praises of evil's demise.
See the sunset through glorious eyes.

Country

I was born and raised in the city, but oh, how I crave the tranquility of the old country scene, the bountiful outdoors, the oak trees swaying in the air, fragrant and clean.

Soil so rich you could plant a penny and yield a million bucks, and Grands works on that old blue Chevy truck.

Family sitting on the front porch gathered to watch the sun quietly fade, sipping on the coldest lemon tonic ever made.

The mosquitoes are buzzing around my head, their piercing proboscises feeding wherever they dare.

That white picket fence is fateful enough, but it does need mending. There are paper fans in every hand with a heat that's not pretending.

Hummingbirds suckle just across the way, and Grandma's bridge group gets together to play.

Every Sunday morn, the chapel is surely bursting. Later we hang out at the creek with Johnny's cousin.

Good times and fine living, potato salad and fried chicken.

Don't forget the biscuits and fresh collard greens. Yes, that is what down-home country means.

To lie back easy and put your feet up. Wow, you know, when I really think about it, the city just sucks.

Rain

I love the sound of the rain rushing down my windowpanes.

I love the way the sparkling drops gather together. Rain is my favorite type of weather.

Pouring against my umbrella and across every rooftop. I sometimes wish it could go on forever and never stop.

I love the way the raindrops kiss the fruit. I also love the slushing sound from my boot.

I love the rain when it's in my view. A crude love affair we share. And how about you?

On the rain I float my favorite paper ship. And oh! how I love those salty drops upon my lips.

I love the rain on a hot summer day. I also love watching the kids as they splash about so gay.

I love the rain; it's wealth straight from heaven, a bucket of liquid gold I've loved since I was seven.

I love the way the rain washes away my blues and the way a steady downpour has no particular tune.

I love how it soaks me from head to toe, how it almost always joins the wind when it blows,

How it has always loved me, has always been there. What a marvelous friend in the rain we all share.

This Is My Body

Today I open my nostrils and I breathe in. Yes, I can feel that it's life.
I feel the tiny pumping in my chest, its steady flow racing through my body, every vein.
I feel that strong and solid structure within me holding it all together,
And I feel an amazing pooling of water that is hydrating my every thirsting muscle under my skin.
I feel the textured cover that drapes it all, wrapping its way around my bones, fitting like a glove. I feel my eyes as they see, my tongue as it tastes, and my hand as it touches, and I feel that my heart shows love.

This is my body. Though imperfect, this is me.

I Have

I've believed in something yet nothing at all. I've enjoyed the laughter of children both big and small.

I've watched the stars in the wee hours of the night. Once I saw an eagle spread its wings broad then take flight.

I've admired a man they once called king, a doctor, a preacher, his words a many-splendored thing.

I have swum in the oceans of my vivid imagination, have visited the shores of Hawaii and Greece needing no invitation.

I have pondered words of wise men now cold in their graves, but I have never made love more than twice in one day.

I've shed tears for those I have never known, and over time and the withering years I have grown.

I have laughed heartily and at the top of my lungs. I have slept on a park bench but never fired a gun.

I've felt the chill of many snowflakes on the tip of my nose and the warmth of white sand between my toes. I've wept alone many times and again. I'm not a perfect person, but who is without sin? I have danced and danced until my legs were numb, bathed in the glowing miracles of God's Son.

I've been blessed, and my life has been spared.

I've loved and adored, and truly I've cared.

An abundant life I have lived. I awoke this morning praising these gifts.

Horizon

The awakening horizon cascades off the lake. An angelic fawn grazing stops to take a drink.

Gale winds prance in a vividly circular motion, their scent positively, absolutely an intoxicating potion.

Blue skies and tranquil sunsets.
Mother Nature. We are faithfully in her debt.

Disaster

The lightning flashes and the thunder soars, the earth shaking and the ground roaring.

Mighty flames emanate from below, sharing the brooding blaze, while grumbling souls yell at the top of their voices.

The rain pours with a vengeance and the rapids erase every shore as the world weeps in desperation, crying out no more.

Mud-soaked feet trample in the night, people in fear fleeing to reach the safety of a mountain's height.

Exploding concrete and twisted steel covers every path. There's hardly enough provision anywhere to last.

Bending daisies and screaming branches take flight as if they have wings. Bitter hailstones plummet to the ground as mighty as past kings.

Tiny pellets singe the flesh like an army of hollow bullets. Sticky with blood, the air stinks like so many overrun toilets.

Standing waves of grand proportion walk the land, human and beast succumbing to what is ultimately evil's plan.

Alone in a Crowd

Alone, lost in a room filled with people, I am someone whose name everyone knows and whose names I know. Wine and spirits greet every desirous hand and the awaiting tongues of most. In the gathering of air, all raise their glasses in good cheer—a toast.

The music is playing at a pleasant enough volume, just above the din of casual chatter.

Folks gorge themselves on salad and pie, while there in a quiet corner of the room goes I.

Though I'm surrounded both in front and behind, I'm alone, lost in a room filled with people. This is fact.

Faceless Voices

I look outside my window, staring at the world that is around me. I turn to watch inside the four walls that surround me.

I stare at the light bulb above me, not admiring its brightness, simply taking its lively glare for granted.

I sit in the same red seat every morning as I have my lukewarm cup of grounds and that fateful single slice of cinnamon raisin bread.

The room is filled with voices, some old, some new.

They reach out to me with their many opinions, their visions.

But there are no faces devoted to those many voices, much like specters in my midst.

They feed my brain with suggestion, wisdom, and wise references, things that they want me to know and to convey to others.

Sometimes I'm transported to other worlds on the words of faceless messengers.

Other times I descend, listening in complete awe, my mouth wide open and my ears too.

Stuffed, swollen with information, my head is expanding every moment I must write.

I jot down the words, the thoughts, and even the visions the faceless have shared with me, intended for all to know.

Politics the Deceiver

To you hardheads, you political king's men, you who make the rules that fuel people but who never follow them,

The people are fed up with all your lies, your broken promises, and your dirty laundry list.

You are filling your purses with every dime you can steal while the whole time pretending you're for the people.

Only you benefit, and they have no gain. With your pockets full of ample wealth, the poor don't enter into the plan.

Simply collateral damage, those who fall by the wayside. Still you speak your false words as the many continue to die,

The hungry, the destitute, those without shelter. You kings line your pockets, which get fatter and fatter.

The notches on your belts broaden while the needy are thinned. Where is your heart, man, and where has it been?

The house's corruption is spreading like the flu. Notice that the ones affected are certainly not you.

You eat cake, drink champagne, and rest nicely in your easy chairs. The outsiders, the less fortunate, scrimp and scrape for every little bit of something they can call theirs.

Where is the fairness, and why does it hide? How long must these vehicles, our brothers, collide?

This political machine is getting away with murder. Justice's tears fall away every day as these politicians insult her.

Politics the deceiver, the liar, the thief, a political boys' club, a bank for thieves.

Disease

The duration of the MRI, radiation, chemo, and pills seemingly has no length. I call on Dr. Hope, Dr. Faith, and Dr. God: "Please give me the strength."

Sometimes I feel I'm not going to make it. My body, my mind, can barely take any more of this.

In the morning I wake my stomach.
It greets my toilet. At night I'm burdened by terminal self-regret.

The weight of this condition bites so heavily, not just for me but also even for those who love me.

The cure is hard and my pain harder, but my understanding, my wisdom, has gotten broader.

I know what it is to need someone's help and to lean on the Father, whose love I have felt.

I have felt him moving steadily inside me, guiding me to the light so that I may see,

Bidding me, "Don't you ever give up. No, girl, you have a lot more living to do."

The Promise

He came to us with the Word written upon his tongue, words of power and a peace that strikes like a gun

Moving through us, something to be reckoned with. His plan is to fill the clouds, our heavens,

And make it a place of life, song, and widespread joy, with a place at the Father's table for every girl and boy.

I am giving praise to the Most High, he who made his kingdom in the sky,

He who kisses away the war and pain, whose splendid and unconditional love is always the same,

Whose battles he has already won, who sent his only begotten Son,

Who lifts us up always when we fall, the Father on whom we call.

The world around us is turning upside down. We feel shaken from our solid ground.

When the way seems dark and even bleak, when our bodies suffer and our spirits are weak,

And when we don't know what in the world we're going to do, the Father is there to pull us through,

Waving a light to brighten our path, rescuing our souls, setting our minds free at last.

Gossip

Delicately whispered sentences were heard by those with curious ears.

The gossiping hand of those hidden fears

Is a lesson that should we all learn. One carrying a story has a tongue aching to burn.

Over time what is truth often diminishes as the tale turns from beginning to finish.

What is told isn't what was said.
What began as a tail quickly becomes the head.

Spinning the boundaries of what is truth fuels a lie's burden,
Cutting the veritable throat of proof.

Missing You

Many I've known who are gone now, having left me behind. O Lord, how I miss them all every day and all the time.

I miss all the times we shared and how we laughed and sometimes cried.

Now all I have left is this damned sadness inside.

Yes, there are pictures that remind me of you, the things you used to say, the things you used to do,

But it's not the same. I can't hear your sounds or see that walk of yours when we'd hit the town.

It's so hard to let go, to say goodbye. Since you left, it's as if a part of me has simply died.

You always remembered my birthday; you would bake a cake. I recall that when you would get worried, your hands would always shake.

You always made me feel special, and I knew you loved me; I could tell.

You brought me my first two-wheel bike, sat up with me when I had bad dreams at night.

You surely were the best cook in town, and oh! how on Thanksgiving we'd throw down.

You were the best. I miss you dearly. I would give anything in the world to have you near me,

To brush my hair, to hold my hand, to love me as only a grandmother, a friend, can.

Hopeless

Embarking on snow-covered terrain as the darkness of night rises, enduring the extreme elements where there's no help to find us.
An avalanche of discontentment quickly unfolds, and the dark story of other such stories is foretold,

The story of all those who clung desperately to vision's breath of life against a cold so chilling that such dreams were denied,

A place where dear preservation raised its ample fist to fight, giving death's grip no satisfaction, no delight.

A wintry storm vents, seeking retribution.
Its winds know no conclusion.

Nature's punishment is served to the guilty, to the intruder, and into the selfish hands of the earth's polluter.

The bluster and blister of an icy grave awaiting what was once a lively gaze.

Towers of white and mounds of fluffy gloom. There's no escaping this jaw of certain doom,

Stretching into the realms of infinity, maybe beyond. Drawing from the beasts the weakness of the heart and mind,

This place where even death does grieve and where no longer is sweet life perceived.

Untitled

There are times when I am lonely by myself and I speak up way loud as if I'm speaking to someone else.

There's no one to say good morning to, or
Share a cup of coffee with, or go through the mundane ritual of dinnertime with. The only voices heard or footsteps sounding against the grains of the hardwood floor are mine.

Because there's no other to saturate the walls of this house, I've befriended a dusty little mouse.

He waves his thin tail sporadically as he greets me, his eyes filled with an expectation that seems to say, *It's time to feed me.*

Untitled

The days are long, and they go on forever, time endless. O how I wish that I had someone to share the time with. O how'd we would spend it,

No longer alone and adrift on an empty vessel all the day through. A body was never meant to be alone, but to share connections most true,

A divine togetherness with one close beside: a marriage wholly entwined, the two joined as one to abide.

I

I feel no pain,
I see no ugly,
I know no rejection,
I have no love.

I do not hate,
I cannot worry,
I reject no understanding,
I refuse suffering.

I realize I am.
I center my uniqueness.
I pray on both knees.
I rest, I work, I breathe.

I, I, I. And what the hell about me?

Untitled

There are scars that cannot be erased,

A heart that cannot be embraced,

A life that only seeks space,

A being compromised not by rules or race,

A lobster dinner she has yet to taste,

Champagne he dares not to waste,

A life that spins rapidly with utter haste,

And this is life, my case.

We

All of us have borne the burden of loss, the pain of its jagged edges its cost.

Those weeks of recollection, the file of memories shared. There are the ups and downs, the ins and outs, of what is and isn't dared.

Weeping brows and hanging hearts for the good, now simply longing, spending the moments apart.

The missing of so many happy times, loss replacing the smiles, the joy now forever turned to dismay.

A permanent emptiness now hovering above the wind. Where once our story began is now its farewell, the end.

We all have borne the burden of loss, the chilling sadness that bites like frost,

The burden that pulls at our threads, unraveling us like twine, tugging at us always as if it walks through the corridors of our very minds.

Break

Headache trembling. The earth is spinning. Day is night; night is day.
I can't tell the end from the beginning.

My feet hurt. I am just so very tired of walking. Where are my shoes,
and why aren't you talking?

My bedroom is a prison, a cage, you see.
Help me, someone help me, to ease the rage there be.

My friends, where are they? And where do they hide? Are they waiting
somewhere on the other side?

I must cool my thoughts. My brain is about to explode. My head feels
jammed with a godawful load.

Questioning myself and everything I have come to be,
Even the face in the mirror. Who is that? Is it truly me?

Confusion, frustration, too many hours in jail. Why doesn't somebody,
somebody, end my insanity and post my bail?

Dear Diary

I won't lie, it hurt me when you said we can never be together again. It was as if a hole had been blown through my body, straight to my core. I believe, think, that I put on a brave enough front, when inside I was crumbling into tiny pieces. After we parted, my eyes were so wet that I could not see, and my breathing so labored that I it hurt to breathe. I feel separate from all I thought defined me, us.

I'm broken, chipping away like so many boulders crashing from the highest cliff. All I have known since forever is her, her smile, her laugh, and those sweet lips I'd grown to adore.

How do I move past this when, like hardened concrete, I'm suspended in a vacuum of time?

I cannot move forward, and at the very same time I cannot go back.

So here I and my broken heart stand, petrified, clinging to my memories, our memory. Some of the memories are good, and some are bad, but still they will always remain rigidly planted inside the vessel that houses our story for all, and beyond all, of time's expectation.

Prophecy

Demons disguised by using the wings of angels, fooling humanity with their wizardry and their healing. But all the while the humans' blessed souls the demons are stealing.

Humankind, your eyes are blinded by the sheer glimmer of gold. Dazed, you ignore the doctrine, the creed ages ago foretold.

The whole world's a fashion show and an endless pit of "Oh me." Men and women are only concerned about indulging themselves, the "How much?" and the "Plenty."

The knife he sticks in his brother's back will soon be stuck in his own. Pathetically he does not hesitate, posting, with a smile, a picture of his crime on his dear phone.

His dedication is an homage to his false god, so ignorant to the true Son's teachings, how he died.

They deny purpose and drown in a tide filled with regret's bait. There's no peace without repentance. The soul cries, "It's too late!"

The Unwanted

Please get off my back. Stop harassing me. Get out of my face. You're stealing my joy, you see.

Give me some space. Take two steps back. Learn your place. This feels like a heart attack.

Hey, take your hands off me. Why are you so angry? Let's have lunch. I'll make tea.

Today you say you love me, tomorrow you only hate, wearing your prizefighter's gloves, which land on my chest with all your weight.

This is killing me. I don't think you care. I just want to be free, free from your hateful eyes that deadly stare.

Abuse is your paint; my body, your canvas. My tears have no date, and fear forever finds us.

I Do Fall

Wake up, people. Put down your arms, those ghastly weapons of destruction meant only to harm.

Raise your eyes, your hands, to brotherly love, mimicking the Father who resides above.

Don't walk away. Can't you see that we hunger, that our world, this planet, has been torn to bits, blown asunder?

Turn not our backs to ones in need, nor deny those empty souls desperate to feed.

To understand, to walk together in stride, bursting tainted views and distorted pride,

Cursing what is good, what's right and pure, for what matters not and those things unsure.

The bonds of family, the fabric tattered, even ripped. I can't breathe. God help me, I'm choking.

Devastation, manipulation lacking in creation, it reeks; it burns the brutality of temptation.

Distortion and disfigured reality doth reign. Is this how things are supposed to remain?

On my knees I do fall, my bloodstained face to the ground. I scream, "Freedom for all!"

Perfect

See my mountains, their beauty and awe, and my sky, a painted picture in a dream I saw.

The fragrance of lilies and lilac tangle in the midst, youth's sweet effervescence like a portrait that insists.

Blades of green cover the ground as a freshly prepared bed for all to lie down.

Joy and bliss doth fill the air,
A slice of heaven for all to share.

And the sun peeps down to kiss the earth, its grace as innocent as the measure of a new birth.

Yes, pure and simple, this is a king's delicacy, a gentle wind calming the seas, a perfect world designed for thee.

My sky a painted picture in a dream I saw. The mountains with their beauty. I close my eyes in awe.

Steady Rising

I am fending for myself now, but I'm not by myself. I have my Lord God and all his help.

He lifts me on those days, in those moments, when I think I can't go on. He gives me the strength every day with his song.

He lets me know I'm cared for and that always I'm loved, sending down his angel to watch over me, protecting me from above.

There is no doubting his power or strength. In like manner, from above, he pours out his gifts,

Knowing my true heart and what is inside. I thank you, Lord, for your Son's sacrifice and how he died.

A fake love tried to break me, but it seems all that I've lost is pride, because in my Father's worthy arms I have only continued to thrive.

I have become a better me, growing wiser. It's all because of you, Father; this I surely know.

Wiping away the pangs of all those lost years, the heartbreak, and every fallen tear,

I haven't lost anything, no. In fact, I have gained a new life, a new juncture. As when mining for gold, I've struck a new vein.

On my chin for ten I lie, but a hundred more I stand. You never know what's out there for you, what God's plan is.

I Dream in Pastel Colors

As far back as I can remember, I have more than enjoyed the giddy sound, the pleasures, of laughter. I have always admired a star-filled, brightly lit summer sky, and I love to be closely nestled beneath a cozy blanket on a chilly winter's eve with a special someone.

I dream in pastel colors of a place, a fantasy paradise, and of bedding down in a place wild and pure. I dream of seeing the bluest of plunging waterfalls as it cascades down, along with ample mountains, their winding curves and crevices.

I have always loved romance's fiery electricity, the very moment when our lips would meet for the first time, our two hearts beating, pumping as loudly as a bass drum, the pounding melody of passion's unbridled release.

I've always loved the idea of sharing a beautiful life with another and painting our love story across the world, on every corner we meet, filling our lives with poetry, long walks, the intrigue of travel, and a million picnics. I believe in family built on a godly foundation and in an honest love for my brothers and sisters around the globe. And, my friends, I believe in you, because all lives matter.

Just One More Chance

I call you but you do not answer.
All I want is another chance with you,

A moment, darling, to state my case,
Some time to catch up in the race,

Another day in your arms. I want your understanding. I want you to live up to all our planning.

You claim you love me again, and I hear myself murmur softly much the same.

I wish for you to hit that "back on" button, be a family again, share cousins.

Have lunch with me. Allow me my say. Please let us live to love another day.

Nameless

Pretty girl, pretty woman, don't you know you mean the world to me?

When I am with you, I'm flying high for all to see.

When you enter the room, the patter of my heart is suddenly frozen,

And every bit of me knows that it is you, my sweet, I have chosen.

I have never felt this way for anyone before you.

Every word I'm saying, every breath, is true.

You're my breath and every calm breeze that propels me.

You are the guardian, the gatekeeper of the heaven inside me.

You bring me a bliss that mere words can never define. In my soul we are forever stranded together on love's island.

My love outnumbers all the grains of sand in all the world.

My love is like infinity, a perfect circle.

Like putty, I melt in your tender grasp.
I've searched a lifetime to find you, which I have done now and at last.

The world has blossomed like an orchard of fruit trees with limitless flowers.

For moments spent with you, I cherish every single hour.

The minutes, the hours, your loving kiss. You're all that's wonderful; this my heart insists.

Love me, love me, love me as I love you, and let us dance in love's harmony all our days through.

Girlfriend

Girl, stand up and don't let anyone talk to you as if your head
Is screwed on backward. Hey! Like, you, my girl, don't have a brain
to fill it.

Don't ever allow anyone to cripple you with their petty insults, their
small-minded perceptions, their conceit, or their criticisms.

They did not make you, did not breathe life into that brilliant body
you are wearing.

Surely they cannot break you. Let me go on, please. Don't let those Joes
and those Moes determine your worth and your value, girlfriend. This
is something for only you and God to know.

Don't ever let another trip you up, take you off your square.
You stand up proud, unshakable, in the midst of the greatest storm, the
greatest challenge, girlfriend.

To you, my sister, be aware—yes, aware—of the person you are, the
person you strive to be, even if you are not completely sure who you
are destined to become.

Hold your beautiful head up, stick out your chest, my dear one, and
walk on, strutting your stuff.

You have this, and you have so much to say. Shout, talk, girlfriend.
Talk.
Be heard. Don't you be shy.
Know that everything about you counts for something great.

Let no one steal your shine, your glamour, your grace.

The Lord says you are beautifully and wonderfully made. Wear this. Own it. It's yours. It's you.

My girlfriend, you're a dime, a diamond a queen, a jewel, and a pearl. You are like no one else, girlfriend.
You are that girl.

At the End

Lightning strikes. Rain pours.
Tiny creatures scurry about.

The sun has hidden its velvet glow, and all the earth has lost its sparkle.

The dark, the dark covers every crack and every doorway, its flavor digesting humanity's hopes and dreams with a ravenous endless appetite.

And the dull of this black has slowly devoured the light as if its gleam never existed.

Guilty

There are ghosts in my head. They follow me time and again, taunting me with my every thought. I'm going insane.

Those specters of my past and of so many events, the things I have never told, hidden in my bones, very well-kept.

The ghost is called Guilty, and it brings up all my shame, my memories so vivid that I know each one by name.

Can't take it back, so what am I to do, when it's no lie but absolutely true?

My conscience is a witness that sticks, attached like glue. I can't shake this phantom no matter what I do.

Sitting cozy beside me, my Siamese twin haunts me always with a vicious shrieking from deep down within.

Its ominous laughter, its giggling display, is deaf to my reluctance, my pleading say.

Even in my sleep, this presence still finds me. It is real, its honesty so blaring that it nearly blinds me.

Yes, I being the culprit, I confess my deeds. Now handcuff me, dearest truth, and then we might proceed.

Smile

I smile when I'm happy.
I smile even when I'm sad.
I smile sometimes with joy around others because I'm mad.

I smile with friends,
And I often smile alone.
I smile because I feel like it.
I smile to atone.

I smile when the sun is bright, and I smile with the crescent moon.
I smile sometimes out of place and, yes, sometimes way too soon.

I smile with strangers, people I meet in passing.
I smile when the music plays, and I smile when I'm dancing.

I smile when I'm happy and sometimes even when I'm stressed.
I smile because it's beautiful. I smile because it's what I do best.

Curiosity vs. Discovery

Sitting in my room all day sipping wine. O the many words that cloud my mind.

There are so many words, so much I yearn to say.
I'm pretty sure I was simply born this way.

Tied up in knots, curious to a fault,
My feelings ignite me; they are as powerful as a volt.

I get drunk, but I never stagger. Every minute I'm praying for better,

A better me, a better you, a better day, a moment sober, the perfect words for my unwritten play.

I get headaches; I'm thinking too much.
I would love to have a pretty woman to make love to, to touch,

Someone to talk to, maybe express myself with, write a tell-all book of everything I have felt.

Maybe I'll smoke a cigarette, though I have never smoked—but more than likely on its vapors I'd choke.

I should take a trip, one of long traveling, and see some things I have never seen before or dabbled in,

Unload the stresses, the strain of that which is me, learn what freedom from myself truly might be.

Carpenter

He bled, this carpenter called Jesus, for our sins, and then he died. And in three days he rose again.

So many amazing miracles did this Christ preform, his parables meant to save our souls, shelter humankind from death's storm.

Filled with God's joy, his forgiveness, and his love, Jesus was first a boy and then a wise man, an angel from above.

No greater sacrifice or love could we ever know. He's the instructor, the coordinator of how the body must go.

We are protected by his mercy and his grace. His spilled blood has saved the human race.

Call on Jesus. He'll always be there for you in your struggles and disillusion. Your burdens he'll bear.

In the darkness the Lord will bring you light, lifting the weight of your every plight.

He's your friend, your salvation. He is Lord. His walk is the greatest story ever told.

Ghetto Palace

The rain falls, hitting like bricks of my ragged rooftop.
I see the failing shingles as one by one they collapse.
I also see a bird with her chicks, which she struggles not to drop.

This structure is old, feebly bearing the weight of its many-numbered days, its better footing now lost to the bending of age as it is in need of repair. It has failing joints, rotting woodwork, and separating mortar.

Still I'm grateful to have, to own, my ghetto palace, this crumbling tenement I for so long have called my home, its walls worn and desolate, stretching out their arms toward this common place.

When Will It Change?

Last night there was a shooting. A young boy was left in critical condition. The morning is gloomy, and hearts hang ever so pitifully.

When will it change? Our world has been rearranged.

The breath of life is not taken seriously, is gambled with every day. How much more must we take of this, and where is our better way?

When will it change?

The daily corruption of children, the molestation of a darling mother. This has to end, this father against brother.

When will it end?

My people are lying in the streets and begging for food. Murderer—hey, you, preying on the weak—I have had enough of your hateful attitude.

When will it end? When will it change?

"To arms!" is the outcry, a woman shouting at the top of her lungs, "Free God's people, and please put down your guns!"

When will it change?

Go away, you gossiper, you backbiter, and your crew. Up with the intended regime, something kinder, gentler, new.

Let's find the peaceful part of ourselves and a place we can all share. Stop pushing it all away with your doubt. Gather together. Let's learn to care.

Powder the Illusion

I'm powerful, soaring high above the clouds. This is amazing, I mean, these new wings I've found.

I can do anything. I can't fall, so high above my body, I can see it all.

My blood rushes through my veins.
Fire—this feeling is totally insane.

Where have you been? I've searched all my life for something this awesome in those tiny bits of white.

Give me my cape. I'm Superman, bulletproof. But save all your concerns and your boring truth.

I've never felt so strong, so alive, so well. So all you haters can go straight to hell.

Let me stay up. I'm never coming down, having these white wings, these bits of white I've found.

I can fly forever, and always I will, just as long as I can afford the dope man's bill.

Do You Remember?

Do you remember the last time you were happy and you really smiled? Do you remember when you had no need to pretend and joy filled your soul all the while?

Do you remember the last time you had fun, took a long walk, bathed in God's sun?

Do you remember the last time you were in love, held hands, or relaxed untroubled by Corona's buzz?

Do you remember when you were five, or your best friend when you were nine, or the first time you could actually drive?

Do you remember the best day of your life? And what about all that motherly and fatherly advice?

Do you remember growing up and how being a kid how sometimes really sucked?

Do you remember your chores, washing dishes, believing in fairy tales, and making wishes?

Do you remember all your worst nightmares, the closet monster, your scariest fears?

Do you remember big hugs and your face full of kisses, how from time to time you miss this?

Modern Age

It bites, it eats, it swallows,
This spirit of souls, rent ever hollowed.

A device meant only to devour day by day, every minute on the hour.

Take, take, taking, but always giving less of a care that knows not and offers no forgiveness.

A frowning culture void of tenderness, fraught with fear, and still very careless.

This culprit goes by the name of the modern age.
In this age are a people whose limits have no gauge,

A folk utterly consumed with self, caring very little for anyone else.

Self-centered, self-serving are they,
Opposed to seeing life any other way,

Their own selfishness and overblown acclaim
Serving as their own destruction and steadily crippling them just the same.

Winters

The winters of my years go on beyond fifty. I was born in a time when kids used phrases such as "way out" and "nifty."

My years know of a time when music was considered golden and when a man and his word were never parted, never broken.

Gentlemen tipped their hats, pulled out chairs for a lady. Politicians shook the hands of their constituents and kissed all the babies.

Family was the most valued thing in all the world, more priceless than silver and more splendid than gold.

My winter's length suggests a condition of knowledge procured, and upon my brow are creasing wrinkles, evidence of the ages I've endured.

Of my winters, some were good and others not so grand. Now that I am nearing my end, days slip away like falling bits of sand,

Each bead a memory, a picture of many winters lived, volumes of my life, those days, those leaves of so privileged.

Fall

I can hear the dog barking out back, and I'm thinking to myself, *Why is this guy in such a frisky state?* But I move on. Then I notice the faint cracking sounds upon my roof and the wet glassy beads of soft, crystal-like raindrops as they gently hit my window. I watch those beads melt and slowly trickle down, then vanish into the worn and rotted wooden frame of my window. I see the fall; it's all around me, everywhere I look.

It is the brown and amber leaves covering my door front, the faded and shriveled remaining bits of once green blades of grass just across my street. It's the neighbors' young'uns all dressed up in their warm yet moderately priced casual cardigan sweaters, and it's that fall sky all made up and kissed with an arrangement of many colors.
What a brilliant, powerful emotion this blessed season brings, and such tasty delicacies as apple cider, rum, warm cocoa, and hot apple pie covered with a heaping scoop of rich, black-beaded vanilla ice cream.

There's the awesome unforgettable aroma of a roasted turkey with all the trimmings on Thanksgiving Day.
O how I love the incoming note of wintry blast that the fall brings.
I love the fall.

Rochelle

I see the movement of my tiny lips, but silent are the words.

I hear the singing of song, but where are the birds?

I feel the not so subtle bang of a constant heart's repeat, and I sense the trampling of many rushing feet.

I have felt the sun's rays, both cool and hot. I know people are loved, and I question why I am not.

I know that I live, but I know not from where this knowledge came. I know I have a mother and that she gave me my name.

The End

Darkened days and endless nights, tear-filled eyes and screaming hearts, dear destiny steadily playing its part.

The taste of corruption is bittersweet, and its fill is vile.
But the weak thirst for its flavor as they bed down with denial.

Redemption

My heart opens though my eyes slam shut to the madness. My feelings sense the world and all its sadness.

I see the pain many bring to others' lives, and I see how foolishly these people run, not knowing that they cannot hide from time,

For time and their suffering is the payment for their deeds past. The reign of evildoers will not last.

A day of reckoning soon will come, and with it the power of the Father and his Son.

Dawn

The hot winds of summer blow. The bluebird sings tunes I don't know.

Strange faces appear at every turn, and the sun stares with eyes that burn.

Love is wondering, seeking an escort, a tender kiss, a gentle thought.

Life indeed is a divine companion, its taste sweeter than one could imagine.

You embrace life with a passion to go on, saying goodbye to the emptiness and hello to the dawn.

Light

Steadily walking toward the light, I still can't see, as if something is covering my eyes, blinding me.

The glare is so close, almost at hand, but the closer I get, the more the distance seems to expand.

Walking, walking until my shoes are none, reaching for the light of the Most Powerful One.

The light of true vision, truth, a life lived knowing the superior height.

The door to my salvation and my Father's praise; to live forever in his tender loving ways.

Road to Excellence

They go on forever, those roads of cobblestone, as do the statues and monuments of praise.

My love is like those monuments, built to last forever and to strengthen with each passing day.

You are a victim of excellent beauty, like a perfect sunrise and sunset giving life to me. You're gentle in a way that no occupant of earth could ever forget.

Neither your brilliance nor your kiss from the stars, nor you having been a dove in a former life, explains your grace.

To this empty soul, you've opened doors. In my heart for you there's a permanent place.

Happiness

There's a peace that surrounds happiness, a protective shield that uplifts us,

A winged smile that brightens our darkest days, bringing direction to a world of cross ways.

Happiness is but a rainbow, a walk in the woods. To lie in a meadow, to hold hands, when two lips meet—this treasure called happiness is ever so sweet.

For Love's Sake

Give unto me the boundaries of your soul to love and to cherish, to have and to hold.

Limit not the fires of your lust. My beautiful darling, you must.

I have but one love, and it is you, my jewel. Without you, what am I to do?

I carry this yearning deep inside for surely all this love I can't hide.

I love the mist of your breath, warm and sweet. Delightful you are from head to feet.

Delay no more for it's your tenderness I ache for. I want you to bring me kisses at night, to make my world seem right, to bring me passion like never before. It's you, my darling, whom I adore.

My love is as great in number as the pearls in heaven's gate. Please say you'll forever be mine, for love's sake.

Is It Something You've Done?

A stream of tears flows from your face. Your head hangs in disgrace.

Your grief seems more than you can bear. Consumed you are by fear.

A host called guilt rides your back. Like a headhunter, he attacks,

A cannibal devouring you whole, his stomach a bottomless pit of hot coal,

Burning until you're well done. Tell me, is it something you've done?

A Pain in My Soul

For the million tears I do cry, I ask myself over and over, "Who am I?"

A silent rage and a heart of pleading. O God, why doesn't someone help me?

Tell me what it is that I have done wrong to be left here in this place all alone.

The hands of many substances have taken me full, my only escape being a heavenly tool.

Finding myself is a task indeed. Your mighty grasp is all I need.

Nighttime

The streetlamps are burning ever so bright, cutting through the dark and eerie night.

There goes the familiar howling of a neighbor's dog as he barks at the moon then growls amid the night's fog.

At the window an old woman with curious eyes stares as her dearest Henry lies fast asleep without a care,

Resting softly against the darkness of a pitch-black sky, a million tiny stars shining with no particular reason why.

A stray kitty licks away, perched on that same ragged fence night and day.

And a lost raccoon through the quiet street creeps; from car to car, this stripe-tailed creature swiftly leaps.

I'm a Black Woman

My hair is nappy. My skin is dark. Do these facts deem me as less, as apart?

Born in a white man's world, I live his hell. Still, my Bible tells me that I must forgive.

The ghetto is all I see, and pangs of hunger I have known, yet still I managed to become full-grown.

Now I know what I am: a black woman. I say it boldly, proud of my heritage, my Negro ways.

So, like a uniform of honor, I wear this black skin, my head so high that even my nappy hair blows in the wind.

My color, my hair, and my music are all loud. I'm a black woman, and she sure be proud.

Glory

Glory, glory, beautiful glory.
Come sit a spell and hear my story.

A mustard seed thriving to reach great heights, though frustrated, worn, and weary, ever makes its relentless strides.

Glory, sweet glory, may your colors wave bright. Persecuted, imprisoned, you still fight a glorious fight.

You suffer pangs of injustice, though you cry no claim to fame. Oh dear, sweet glory, we salute your name.

Tormented, long-suffering, weary, and sore. Confused and desperate, sometimes that much more.

Captured, locked into a claimed affliction, and as empty as a vessel without ambition.

Colored burdens weigh heavily as their souls weep for God's glory.

Many are wearing sorrow's shackles like a noose around the neck. While the spirit cries mutiny, the flesh swabs the deck.

Now I am but a servant to that which has challenged me and stolen my joy.
I have been left merely a vagabond, as insignificant as a child's broken toy.

Love Is

Love is such a powerful word, but it is seldom spoken, too seldom heard.

Spoken from the lips, it might be true, but when it comes from my heart, it is more praised by you.

Sometimes love is so toyed with that it leaves behind a cripple, but amazingly, like molten rock hardening to be stronger, it seems to triple.

Love does pass but is never forgotten, like a delicate cream always rising from the bottom.

Sonia

Never such a love will you ever find,
Never a love as true as mine. Search throughout eternity as you may,
and beyond all of humankind, but seek no more a love so true neither
near nor far behind.

I am here to set light upon your blackest days and to shower your
cloudiest moments with a love to praise.

Fear me not for I mean you never any harm, only passionate lovemaking
and a fool's charm.

Offer me the pure depths of your tender heart, a length that love can
reach.
Show me all the knowledge that your fluttering passions do teach, and
lend me the warmth of your body, your soul. I'm yours forever, darling,
to have, to hold.

My waking anatomy awaits, filled with frustration, impatiently wanting
the throbbing of your appreciation.

Never a love such as this shall you ever find,
And never a passion as true as mine.

When

When I touch you, my eyes see how lovely true beauty can be.

When we kiss, my heart knows a feeling that by day seems to grow.

When held tight in your arms, my body swallows the essence of your forbidden charms.

And when we walk, you hold my hand, making me feel like no one else can.

When I close my eyes at night, you come to me, caressing, in such a heavenly sight.

When we make love, it is paradise for two, alone on a tropical island, me and you.

Sun

I see the sunshine, its presence, when it comes and when it goes.

I admire the sun's orange hue, its heavenly glow.

Feeling the heat of the sun every day when it's beaming, I love the way it touches my skin. Its smile is always gleaming.

I love how the sunshine nurtures, restores, and brings new life,

How through its eye all life thrives.

The sun follows me wherever I am, and I know I can count on the sunshine's vision forever to guide me.

Though one body, it speaks to me like many voices from its place there above the clouds. Its music visits me like a beautiful song playing out loud.

Contentment

A winter's day finds me walking through the snow as it covers my street. I cannot help but notice the crisp sloshing sounds below my every footstep and the way my sneakers sink deep between the white's many flakes. I can feel the cuffs of my pant legs as they wrestle with the cold and the wateriness of winter's blister. The accumulated frozen foliage bites as I stroll slowly by. Just for now I don't have a care in the world.

I engage the fresh brisk air that surrounds me. It tickles the long hairs inside my now ruby-red nostrils with my every inward breath.

I listen to nature's music. Her sounds are everywhere I turn, but still there are those special moments when I witness and hear nothing except the subtle yet powerfully consistent beating of my own pounding heart. It goes *thump, thump, thump* over and over like the once reliable ticking of my granddad's big clock, never missing a single ticktock, its consistency like my heartbeat, most hypnotic, compelling me to listen. But I don't mind because I know with unblemished certainty that this is life, the sheer beauty of liveliness racing through my every bone, all my extremities. Yes. And always I know that this beautiful winter of my life is wrapped in the dear arms of utter contentment.

The Beauty That Is You

Heavenly, I have gazed into the amazing thing that is you, always anticipating the moment when our single souls would become two.

Spellbound by the sensuousness of your penetrating kisses, my passions burn inside me and I know truest bliss.

The blackest night cannot hide your vivid smile as its sharpness leaves even the sunshine in bitter denial.

For your presence in my life, I would cross an ocean and climb the highest mountain. I would bear the scorching heat of the hottest desert, and in your image I'd create the grandest of fountains.

I would bow at your feet and fulfill your every request, then I would pray that of me you don't think any less.

For your love all these things I would surely do, merely to be lavished by the beauty that is you.

Do I?

Do I bravely imagine the softness of your mouth against mine, the flowery scent of your breath so divine?

Do I challenge the black velvety pools that house your eyes, or the yearning within me to provoke your love even if for but one time?

Do I dare imagine the delicateness of your every touch or the luminous laughter I have grown to adore so much?

Do I chance the shimmer of your every flowing hair, the eternal cry that calls me again and again to take a dare with one so fair?

Do I dare imagine you to love only me, to share a desire built to last for all eternity?
Do I?

Those Steps

My two leg know those steps, all twelve, from the very top to the last one at the winding bottom.

This ladder, those steps, my legs know when I am well winded and also when they themselves are exhausted.

My legs know every creek and every crack of those still richly painted mahogany stairs,

The many chips from the years of use, those places where the paint is flaking away just a little more, most every day.

My legs know the steps that are bent and sunken and those that have borne the weight of so much traffic year after year.

My legs know my most favorite step to stop on and take the occasional breath before committing to the rest of this body's climb.

My legs know those steps in the cold and in the heat of day. When it is dry out or even moist, on my good days and on the bad ones too,

My legs often tire of their use, but still somehow they manage.

My legs know the broken last stair best of all. I recall the heaviness of Mom's bed's headboard as it crashed down hard on the staircase, leaving the steps, as they've been for years now, in disrepair. They always wiggle just a bit when I climb to remind me.

Yes, my legs know those steps. I think to myself, *I believe I know them like an old friend, those steps, those steps.*

Cold, Cold, Cold

Cold, cold, cold. Such a cold day, cold, cold, cold. The kids want to go out and play.

Cold, cold, cold. What a wintry way. Cold, cold, cold. Even too cold to ride in a sleigh.

Cold, cold, cold. What more can I say? Cold, cold, cold on this icy Sunday.

Cold, cold, cold, my December birthday. Cold, cold, cold. My, how chilly is this day.

Cold, cold, cold. If only I had it my way.
Cold, cold, cold on the ocean, watching the continent's equatorial seaway.

Cold, cold, cold. Maybe someday—and cold, cold, cold—I will travel the world's freeway.

Yeah, cold, cold, cold, even on a Monday. Cold, cold, cold; that is it, all I have to say.

Signs

There're everywhere, on every street corner you meet and practically at every light post you may pass.

They're both up high and down low, directing us, telling us where to go.
They tell us where we should tread not, where to go in and come out, and when to stop. They indicate where we should enter and where we should not dare.

They tell us right and left, fast or slow, where we can park, where we must go.

They instruct us, warn us, even entertain us too, showing us where to dine, where to lodge, and how far away we are from the closest zoo.

They tell us where to gas up and where to rest.

All those posted alerts written in choice words provide direction. When written for the handicapped, they show, for example, the parking spaces reserved for our vets.

There are danger zones, roads that are slippery when wet. Some of the signs are bright; some are dark. Some tell of men at work, very sharp turns, and construction work. There are so many signs, but I have yet to see one that ever rhymes.

A Dream

In pure wonder I gazed at her, hardly able to trust my own eyes.

She was very beautiful, a veritable doll come to life.

She made graceful yet vivaciously sweeping motions as she crossed the room.

Her stare met mine. As if to speak from her lips, her eyes spoke.

My compassion leapt internally, and my breast pounded with vigor, sounding with the rumbling zeal of a thousand drum strokes so eager.

I know I love her, adore her, though I know not her name.
This angel is begging to be mine forever. Always her image I shall claim

My spirit is desperate to follow her wherever she may go, like the waters of the sea in continuous flow.

Unfortunately, this woman is a dream. She comes and she goes like a ghost I have never been certain I've seen.

Dealer

See that dude on the street? He be pushing that weed, growing up. Man, does him mom struggle, but it is a dad he needs.

With empty hopes for a better future, he simply follows the green.

Where he comes from, cash is the only thing that has any meaning.

He's shooting the dice and wearing that pawn shop ice, far from being concerned for his own or anyone else's life.

He and his cellmate, they be boys for life, doing a two-year bit more than once or twice.

He wears a cross around his neck blinging with jewels, but he knows no prayers, only how to duck the rules.

And from sunup to sundown his phone is surely ringing, his not being selective of whom he serves as long as his pockets are pinging.

Over his shoulder and behind his back he's definitely peeping,

Troubled by the thought of that nine someday finding him where he's creeping.

With the life he lives, there is always one certainty pending and another person wanting his bread. This speeds up the process of his breath ending.

Hurricane

The waves crash determinedly against the ocean shore, giving way to sandy beaches. The blowfish and the starfish cling to the ocean floor, and the dolphins swim out as far as the sea reaches.

The winds hurl, the waves roar, and the mouth of a watery grave screams out.

The rain pours down without ceasing, shouting, "There is no escaping this cloud!"

Humankind against the elements? There is no contest; the elements surely rule the game.

Where or when nature will strike is anyone's guess. There is nothing with more determination than a hurricane.

Deadbeat Dad

A father is gone and a child is lost. What ever happened to Daddy's girl? Broken promises and a hurt that comes with a cost as she is abandoned to face a man's world.

Living a life of disillusion and of asking why, searching every face she meets,
She cries, "Where is Daddy?", for it is him in every man's eyes whom she seeks.

He doesn't write or even bother. She wonders if he ever cared. You know every girl needs a father. Hell, who ever said life is fair?

A deadbeat dad is what they call him, you know, that man who ran out on his little girl. But to me he was surely a hero within my own make-believe world.

I Ran

On February 1986 I began running the marathon of a lifetime. Who would have ever guessed I'd be telling my story with this rhyme?

I ran and ran. I ran from life, running with no idea where I was going, running recklessly and blind. Daily now I pay the price.

For eleven years I've run this wicked race, searching for the positive in a negative space,

Living on pipe dreams and using game to get by, crying into my pillow at night silently, *Why oh why?*

Why am I running? I question, What is my fear? Could nothing be worse than the person I see in my mirror?

Some call me a coward and even a dropout, but I laugh 'cause I've earned my PhD at the University of Runabout.

My tattered clothes and my empty belly—shit, while some folks wish for gold, I pray, "Lord, pass the peanut butter and jelly."

I have scars that no bandages could ever disguise, and the memories of how I got them will never die.

The dining halls of the pen, that custom-fitted straitjacket, my friend,

Always wondering what it will take. Maybe a coming-out party where the state's coroner is my date?

Lately my running shoes are worn and my back is surely aching. At thirty-one years of age, should my hands be shaking?

I've seen it all, but all the while I've seen nothing. All my life I have just been running.

Now I've run shit out of time, and I'm not completely sure all these words rhyme,

But in case they don't, don't worry. Just consider my message: Slow down, for God's sake. Don't run. There's no hurry.

A Dream

Pausing to take a seat in the wild, I see an oak tree breathe then sigh out loud.

There are animals of all colors nestled close, and the fowls of the earth sing out in verse.

Every blade of grass proudly stands up straight, prepared for summer. O so worthy a date.

A caterpillar has become a butterfly. I wave at the hawk as it flies by.

The ground beneath me speaks, even laughs.
Across the lake, a school of fish take a class.

A dewdrop falls upon my nose as I catch a chill that runs from my head to my toes.

Then up my back I feel a friendly snail creeping, and oh! to my surprise, I awake for I was just dreaming.

Ebony Womanizing

It's 1997. I wear this ebony skin, threatened daily by social discrimination.

And oh! the battles my ebony skin has seen, fighting hard for what being a black woman means.

Unheard are my cries. Unseen is my sweat, my blood, my struggles to exist, my payment. There's no Purple Heart, no awards, no certificates,

And if I'm lucky, maybe on a minimum-wage-paying plantation, I will, like a dog, from nine to five be truly slaving.

As for the system, it throws me a check as if it were a bone, a check that fat politicians say I ain't supposed to get.

They say, "Let the bitch starve, and her children too. She'll find a way. Their kind always do."

A black woman is even a slave to the man whose child she bears, yet her loyalty and his children mean nothing as he walks out the door.

This ebony-skinned woman, now tied to lives she can never deny, God help her, is a black mother with no time to cry.

Mask! A Reflection of Myself

Many tears wash the face I wear.
My eyes are a most unsightly pair,

Cracked, reddened by pain's burden. My weeping sound is as familiar as a melody learned.

To smile is a wish that has not come true, for my days are gray even when my sky shines blue.

Devastation and torment comfort me at night in the darkness of this seemingly winless fight.

I cry, I cry, "Who should rescue a fool such as I from such a fate as to see my soul die?"

I Wonder

Insanity flows through my veins with a poisonous impact, with every day's slimming-of-reality effect.

I am like a drunkard, stumbling through life's remains, my lunacy steadily rearing
Its ugly head time and time again.

There's no cessation to the rage that awaits, yes, to feast on my flesh like a hungry soul facing a needed plate.

Taking every burdensome breath, I find it is an unsympathetic reminder that my soul still lives and that my spirit groans, moaning inside me like the cries of pigs before being slaughtered.

My weeping falls on deaf ears, and my pain is unseen. At the moment of my untimely demise, I wonder who will grieve for me.

Humankind

I long to understand humankind, their ways, their thoughts, their plans.

I long to know why human beings exist and how we will continue to live.

I wonder why human beings cry. Why must we die?

I ponder human reason and the deepest private thoughts. I envision all the wars humankind has fought.

I've seen the blood humankind has spilled, have witnessed the agony of a destiny willed.

I cry now a cry of forever and ever, thinking of all the time human beings may never spend together

With their widespread hatred for one another, and with a sister being down on her brother.

With unity hiding its face, camaraderie has lost its place.

Indeed I do question, Will humankind's pain never end? And will all human beings ever be friends?

The Gift

Our Lord has a rule that is the sweetest by far; it is to love other people just as they are.

It is to place no condition on love given, but to relish the greatness of such a tender feeling

And to appreciate it, to hold majesty firm in our heart of hearts, for love plays a deserving part.

God so gave love for all to feel, to seek after this emotion with all appeal,

For the gift that love presents is worth more than a fat man's weight in gold and is longer in length than all the stories ever told.

Lonely Whispers

Whispers in the night that cry out in fear, shattering the ears of those who dare not hear.

These loneliest of echoes boldly imprison me with the invisible bars of captivity.

I've grown to appreciate companionship so divine while knowing loneliness's sentence of morbid time.

Sitting among the walls, I am unseen, wishing loneliness's burden would stop haunting me.

Loneliness's ghost shows me no sympathy.
I wait. Is this hollow, empty fate my forever bitter destiny?

Printed in the United States
by Baker & Taylor Publisher Services